CW00382551

A VICTIM OF THE IMPERVIOUS

A VICTIM OF THE IMPERVIOUS

A psychological thriller
Contains parts of a true story.

By Caris Poynter

Copyright © 2020 Caris Poynter

All rights reserved

The characters and events portrayed in this book are fictitious. Any similarity to real persons, living or dead, is coincidental and not intended by the author.

No part of this book may be reproduced, or stored in a retrieval system, or transmitted in any form or by any means, electronic, mechanical, photocopying, recording, or otherwise, without express written permission of the publisher.

ISBN: 9798653303746
Imprint: Independently published

Edited by: Ali Iftikhar

To the victims of Sexual Assault and Rape.

Something had changed in her. She was not the same person any-more. She was a Victim of The Impervious.

MAY 2020 | CARIS POYNTER

CONTENTS

PREFACE

Sometime in early 2020, I put pen to paper about the women, the victims, prey of sexual assaults, recipients of rapes, sitting targets of illegal videotaping, and patsy for sex trafficking. I am a mentor and trainer for mental health-related issues, and the necessary concomitant of the anxiety is a concept I have reconnoitred meticulously. I write with natural emotions analogous to that of a character in a real environment.

This book contains some parts of a true story, which makes you wonder what kind of sex predators are out there. Their vivid ways to assault a person are unsought by a sane human. I have shared the real-life encounters with the dark web and how it is being used to buy and sell women in today's lawful world. This story of Louise is awe-inspiring for the victims to come up front and brace the situation. It is never too late to make yourself heard.

INTRODUCTION

During my life long struggle with raising four boys with Tics Disorder, I have encountered a lot more than an average woman of my age. I am certified as a Trainer to advice for Mental Health Patients. My journey with disabilities and fighting for rights has brought to me to a point where I start sharing it with the world. I have written two books, prior to this, about the struggles of mothers.

A Victim of the Impervious is my effort to raise social awareness. A woman does not need to fall into the traps set by sexual predators. The 21st century has brought "technological crimes", which are more than an average woman's grasp. We don't even know what fate has in store for us. However, the crucial part is how do we react to situations like these. The significance of saying Yes or No, staying firm on your ground, doing what the heck you want to do but all with your free will. Nobody - and I mean it in the most practical sense, can force you to do to anything without your Consent.

I would care to hear your stories, if you were a victim and how you came out strong. It is my utmost desire to help anyone who has not yet raised her voice against a private crime. If you have a story to tell, Please reach out to me.

Caris Poynter Email

carishoughton@yahoo.co.uk

FOREWORD

By Ali Iftikhar

My whole career as a hardcore corporate professional had its fair share of coming across sexual harassment cases. Being a Human Resource Management expert, I have witnessed multifold of oppressing events. Glass ceiling and sex discrimination is one thing, but forcing an individual to indulge in sexual activities without full consent is a subject still avoided by many. Ms Poynter has written this fantastic eye-opener for both oppressors and victims.

Louise was the victim of a crime she did not discern. She had been a cautious woman all her life, but that night was one of those stints, where you just could not perceive being subject to a heinous crime. At first, her boyfriend and herself ascertained it as sexual harassment, mild coercion of a sexual nature. Only to find out later, the culprits had wicked plans beyond imagination.

A Victim of the Impervious is a psychological thriller about a British girl who loved everyone around her. Pure of heart, her life was nothing but living to the fullest, one day at a time. This is a record of her struggle against coercion, sexual violence, and emotional torture. The book was penned down to advocate free will and the importance of The Consent.

Caris is a friend and an advocate of social awareness. Her work in this book is painstaking attention to free Consent. As her editor, I have had the opportunity to read this book numerous times, and every time it had a fresh feel to it.

Ali Iftikhar
Manager in the Fashion Industry
Writer and a nature-loving nomad

THE FRIENDSHIP

They met in a cocktail bar on one of those Saturday nights when you just want to dance and drink. He was with two friends, Andrei and Mo, and together they were enjoying the evening.

Lucian was sitting in a corner with his friends when he first saw her. It was the best place in town to spend a weekend night without having to worry about the weekly pressures. She was different and beautiful than the rest. He noticed that she was dancing alone on the dance floor. He watched her closely, admired her beauty, and enjoyed eyeing how lovely she was in her heels.

She looked delighted and confident. At this point, their eyes caught each other, and it felt like everything around them took a pause. Lucian tried to act cool and moved his eyes. In this small moment, she had noticed him admiring her. Then she smiled briefly.

Lucian found the room sparkled with her blushed cheeks. He had a glass of Gin and Tonic in one hand; the other hand was in the air, half-dancing. Lucian had suddenly lost the sense of what was in his glass because of the mesmerising moment. Lucian was so captivated with her beauty that he had forgotten about his friends. Andrei and Mo's heavy accents were silenced to his ears.

Louise would turn around, often smiling at him as he looked in her eyes. Her dance moves had shifted its flow to the cute foreigner's direction, without her knowing. A girl like Louise is always conscious of her surroundings. She was trained by life's hard-hit transitions to look after herself instinctively. However, this was something different. She felt safe, and immediately she was smitten and found him very attractive. Because she did not want to give out any hints yet, she continued to dance.

The curiosity inside Louise's heart was raging. She wanted to know who this person was. She felt a constant, but kind, gaze. Louise would not need to look to tell if someone was watching her or not. She would just know. However, the man with, what seemed to be, his two friends did not raise any alarms in her mind. A sense of safety overcame her as she felt his gaze on her back; an unknown yet deep connection starting to unwittingly form without her knowledge

Known to have uncommon mental health conditions, Louise had developed an urge, a need to explore the suspense. It was not insecurity. It was confusing. After a few songs had been played, she walked briefly to the bar to get herself a drink.

Louise was waiting to be served, and she could feel a presence coming towards her, and as she turned to her right, there stood one very handsome, tall slim, dark-haired, and stubble bearded man.

"Would you like me to buy you a drink", Lucian said.

"That would be nice, thank you". Louise accepted with a kind smile,

"My name is Lucian, nice to meet you", He said after ordering the bartender.

Lucian was overwhelmed with the company of such an amazing woman. He could not believe his eyes, nor could he fathom her beauty. Her long brunette shoulder-length hair, bright wide blue eyes, and the smell of her sweet vanilla perfume, took all of his attention.

They clicked instantly and decided to continue speaking to each other for the rest of the night. Louise was no longer dancing alone; she now had a partner dancing with her on the floor. They dearly enjoyed dancing together and laughing, staring at each other and feeling overjoyed. Whereas Lucian's friends left the bar after having a few drinks as they had noticed that their friend was hooked for the night, and there was no point in waiting for him.

The night ended sooner than she had imagined. Moments spent with Lucian were like a bubble of fantasy. The time had stopped for them. It felt like the cupid had found an aim for its bow. It felt like an instance, which was probably hours. They were also a treat to withstand on the dance floor. The chemistry had taken over the atmosphere. All elements of the periodic table were alive in their time together. But much like all good things, it had to come to an unforgiving end. The gentleman offered to walk Louise home. She decided to play hard to get. Although she intended to not stop, Louise was not going to let her companion feel like scoring an easy trophy. She would not give up her long-formed class in a jiff though it was not easy for her to let go of the first charm. With a heavy heart, they departed the cocktail bar and met the cold night air. He then offered to call her a taxi. She felt biting cold outside, and her skirt was not enough to make her feel cosy. Lucian put his warm leather jacket on Louise. She felt amusingly astonished at his caring gesture, and they exchanged their mobile numbers for future contact. When the cab arrived, Louise returned his jacket and Lucian paid the fare.

The next morning, Louise woke up with an indescribable feeling, the urge to check her phone for any messages or call. It was not the usual thing for her to do as the first thing in the morning. Her phone only showed a text from her sister to remind her that there was a sale going on in the Harrods that she might be interested in. Feeling lost, she finally gathered the motivation to make herself a cup of coffee.

After spending some time watching TV, she was back on checking her phone. At this point, she was sure about whose message she was waiting for. It was definitely the charming guy she had met last night. She could not forget the cologne he was wearing, which was coming from his jacket. Louise did not want to take the first step; it was not her way. She had to wait for the other side to take the lead.

Louise decided to get out of the house to divert her attention. She bought a few things at Harrods that she had wanted to buy. By the time Louise got free, she felt starving. Louise went towards a famous Lebanese restaurant nearby. She had come to the same restaurant a few times before and loved their kebabs. Louise placed the routine order and started looking around the restaurant just to pass the time. She was stunned to see Lucian sitting on a corner table with the same guys who were with him last night. He suddenly felt the gaze and looked back at her with a face full of smiles.

The next moment, he was sitting on her table. Louise tried to act normal, but she could not stop her heart pounding so fast that she feared all the people in the restaurant would be able to hear it. Lucian asked the waiter to serve his food on this table instead. Louise showed concern that his friends might not like it, but he assured her that they would be okay with it, and instead of worrying, she should enjoy her food. He was so gentle in his actions that it made Louise feel so special.

Lucian mentioned that he had forgotten his cell phone at home while rushing to his work in the morning because he had gotten late. He expressed that last night was one of the mesmerising nights in his memory and he wanted to continue seeing her. Lucian suggested that they would meet up at a coffee shop the next day. Still unsure about her feelings, Louise could not stop herself from saying YES.

After Lucian called the taxi, they both waited together. They

5

talked about how lovely the evening was. They wanted to get to know each other more. Louise was delighted to see, it was not just her. It was both sided, and it put her mind to an immense pleasure, although she did not express her feelings yet. Soon after the phone call, the taxi arrived, and Lucian walked over to open the door of the car for Louise to go in safely, being kind and such a thorough gentleman. While seeing her off, Lucian bent over from outside the cab's window and said that he will text her about what time to reach the coffee shop. Louise nodded before the cab drive pressed the accelerator.

Louise could not sleep at night, thinking about the next meet-up. The morning was fascinating to her. She completed her routine chores in no time to have plenty of time to get ready for the date night. Her phone beeped, it was a message from Lucian about reaching the coffee shop by 6:00. For the first time in her life, it took Louise hours to decide what to wear. She wanted to look outstanding, but at the same time, she did not want to portray being overdressed for the date. Louise had to run through her wardrobe for hours before deciding to go for black frilly lace top with skinny jeans. The apparel seemed beautiful and casual at the same time. Louise knew that black colour always made her feel confident and beautiful. She chose black emerald studs to go with it and her Swarovski bracelet that her sister had gifted her on her 20th birthday.

She stood in front of the mirror and wore make-up in a no-make-up-look to appear stunning. She looked at the clock, it was already 6 o'clock. She wanted to be in time for her first date with the handsome man who had caught her eyes since they first met. It was a winter evening, she held her bold coat to wear on top and put on her expensive branded long boots with a heel. Looking at her reflection in the mirror, she knew she could conquer the world with those looks.

When she entered the coffee shop, Lucian was already sitting on a table with his waiting eyes at the door. As soon as he saw Louise, he quickly stood up and walked towards her as to welcome her. He was wearing a casual black shirt with cropped jeans and loafers. Lucian looked like a snake charmer, and Louise could not move her eyes away from him. They were both amused at the choice of the same colour for their dresses as if it was planned. It was a beautiful evening spent together where the aroma of coffee and pastries also smelled romantic.

Lucian told her that he had always wanted to visit the famous Ferris wheel The London Eye with someone special. He asked her if she was available on the next weekend to accompany her. Louise showed her interest in visiting the attraction too and confirmed the plan for the Saturday evening.

Lucian called the taxi as usual and upon arrival, opened the door for her and paid the fare. The gesture that only a true gentleman shows. He kissed her cheek and Louise was all blushed. She waved him bye.

Three days later, it was a Saturday evening, Louise got ready by 5:00 o'clock. Because the place was far away from her house, she needed to leave at least an hour early. This time, Louise had dressed in a long red dress with slits at the bottom ends. She was wearing her red heels and tied her beautiful hair in a French braid. She held her bold coat along with a red clutch when she saw the cab approaching her house so that she could lock the door and got in the cab.

Upon reaching the destination, she looked around for Lucian, as he had happened to be earlier than she was on their first date. She could not see him around, she took her phone out of her bag and was about to call him when she sensed something coming closer to her. It was a beautiful bouquet of Lilies that Lucian was passing towards her. She took it from his hands and smelled flowers. The delicate scent came out of flowers, which made the evening look more beautiful. Lucian was wearing a blue sweatshirt with white lining and black jeans. He was wearing the same loafers as last time, his hair was sleek and combed with hair gel. Lucian looked well-groomed as always. Louise's heart missed a beat while proudly looking at the tall, handsome guy who was there for her.

Lucian held her hand, and they both walked towards the famous attraction that was known to be the tallest Ferris wheel in London and people from all around the world came to see it. Lucian explained to her that he had gone to buy tickets before she arrived. There was usually a long queue at the ticket station, and he did not want Louise to wait there. Lucian's small gestures of care meant a lot to Louise. How could someone be so sweet and caring? She wondered.

The London Eye is a tall Ferris wheel with many capsules attached to it. Capsules are actually the compartments where you could sit or stand and enjoy the view of the spectacular River Thames. The skyscrapers of London and its surroundings from a height of 443 feet while the wheel moved slowly, looks ravishing. It took you to the top in half an hour at a speed of 0.6 miles per hour. Those thirty minutes were unforgettable for both

Louise and Lucian. Lucian had booked a private capsule to them only, which was admittedly more expensive than the usual eight persons' Capsule. It was well decorated from inside with balloons and flowers. There was a bottle of champagne with two wine glasses and some snacks on a small table inside the Capsule. Louise knew that he had put a lot of effort into all these arrangements.

Louise had so far felt so special around him that she started to see him more frequently. They met each other at least twice a week. Usually, it was a dinner night or some drinks at a bar. They both were enjoying their time with each other, and every time Louise met the man, she was more attracted to him. Lucian had a calm yet loving approach towards her.

After meeting for many continuous weeks, they were both exploring their feelings for each other. There was an instant spark between them. Every day, they would meet as much as possible. However, both of them had not decided to take their relationship to the next level yet.

Lucian made her feel loved in particular, and the way that he expressed himself to her was just what Louise was looking for. Lucian would regularly visit Louise at her home in the evening after work. They both would sit in the red kitchen breakfast bar stall, facing each other intimately and romantically; music playing behind and the room filling with love.

He would hold both her hands softly while staring in her bright blue eyes, there was nothing but the truth in his words that he would speak sincerely. Lucian had a habit of telling her daily that she is beautiful. Never a day went by without saying how much he loved her.

One evening, Lucian called her and sounded very excited over the phone. Upon asking, he told her that he had booked the holidays for them to his home country, Russia, for Louise's birthday, which was next month. He had made all the arrangements; he was only waiting for her to accept his offer. The plan was to go there for four days, as they could not stay away from work for longer. Louise was so overwhelmed with this gesture of love that tears came down her face. He suddenly felt her silence and got worried. Louise told him that nobody had ever done this much for her to arrange a trip just for her birthday. It made her feel so precious in Lucian's life.

The next few weeks were spent shopping as the weather was freezing in Russia and Louise needed extra jackets, insulated coats and waterproof footwear. Lucian was always there to guide what was suitable as he was more familiar with the climatic conditions. He told Louise that his family resided in Russia and he wants Louise to meet his grandmother and spend some time with her. Louise felt privileged in doing so. She had no reservations to meet Lucian's family, who had been tremendously kind and gentle towards her. He had brought happiness in her life, and his company gave her enormous delight.

Lucian decided that he will pick Louise up from her house and they both will head for the airport together. Louise was, once again, pleased with his responsible behaviour. He never let her feel alone. It was almost a year since they had met and all these months, Lucian had proved to be nothing but caring, loving and a warm-hearted individual. He had won a special place in Louise's heart, which could never be replaced by anyone in this world.

Lucian picked her up at sharp five in the morning as they had decided. Louise appreciated his punctuality because he had never been late. In fact, he was always 5 minutes ahead of his given time and never made Louise wait for him. Their flight departed the airport at the right time, and Louise's journey began to a new destination that she had never explored. She was hoping to have a memorable time with her stunning companion. The flight was long; they had a nap during the trip but never felt bored as they had each other's company. They enjoyed their moments together in giggles and laughs. Lucian told her stories about his childhood, his family and school friends. Hours passed by in seconds, and Louise did not realise until she heard the announcement of the plane landing in Russia. The breath-taking views outside the window amused her. Once the plane landed, they both picked their hand luggage and moved towards the door.

Lucian had booked a hotel room for their stay; he shifted the luggage to a cab and drove off to the hotel. So far, Louise was inspired by the sights of the city, she was eager to explore more in the little time they had. She was a bit nervous to see Lucian's mother but never expressed her feelings. After taking some rest, they went out for dinner, and Lucian treated her with traditional Russian food. The taste was different but unique, and Louise quite enjoyed it. After dinner, they shared drinks and walked back towards the hotel because it was not far away from the place.

Next morning, the breakfast was served in their room. This time, it was English breakfast, the traditional eggs, toasts with butter and sausages, jam and porridge. They ordered coffee instead of tea. Lucian told her to get ready, as they had to go to see his grandmother, who lived about 2 hours away from the hotel where they were staying. Louise had brought a pure cashmere sweater for her, as it did not seem right to go empty-handed. Her dress was floral, and she wore tights and a scarf because she wanted to look presentable. Lucian gave her plenty of time to get ready so that she does not feel uncomfortable. They left the hotel at 11:00 in the morning. Lucian had rented a car for the journey.

Louise enjoyed the views on the way to Lucian's maternal village. It was on top of a small hill, there was greenery everywhere, and the house looked beautiful from the outside. They reached the house at around 1:00 pm. As soon as Lucian knocked, the door opened wide with an old lady coming out and hugging him in excitement. Lucian held her tight in her arms and kissed her forehead. Louise was amused by this emotional scene, and she knew where Lucian's loving nature came from.

Louise went ahead, and Lucian's grandmother saw her with warm, welcoming eyes. She came closer to Louise and held her hand in her old wrinkled hands and gently kissed the back of her hand. Lucian's grandmother had prepared a delicious meal for them. It was Bolognese pasta with goat cheese and ricotta spinach salad. Louise loved the food, as it tasted delicious, probably because it was made with love. The meal ended with lemon tarts. Louise had never tasted such a divine dessert before. She gave the present to Lucian's grandmother, who was delighted and thanked her for her efforts. She knew very little English; therefore, Lucian interpreted at both sides. Lucian's grandmother gave her a beautiful handcrafted wooden doll beautifully painted in blue and white. Louise loved the present as nothing beats the hand-made presents. They left for the hotel in the evening after spending a memorable day.

It was Louise's birthday the next day; Lucian had not disclosed any plans for her birthday so far. All she knew was that they had to leave the hotel early and travel to a particular place that Lucian wanted to show her. Lucian had proved to be a romantic person. Hence, she had an idea for things to be unique. She wore a black mini halter-neck dress with sequins on the top half, with black heels and a black crossbody bag. Lucian had already gone down to check on the car. When he came back to the room to take her to the car, he was stunned by how beautiful she looked. Lucian was wearing a black suit with a red dress shirt. He had not wished her birthday yet, and she knew that he was waiting for the right moment.

Many eyes followed them when they walked to the car; they appraised their couple, as it seemed they were made for each other. Louise felt the eyes behind them, and it made her feel proud. Louise could not stop thinking about where Lucian was taking her, but he never revealed until they reached a royal palace. He told her, it was The Peterhof Palace and was famous for its honeymoons and romantic dates. The place was terrific and indeed royal. The palace depicted Dutch construction patterns, which was a historical place built some hundred years ago. There were beautiful fountains and gardens all around and inside the castle. Lucian took Louise to the nearby gigantic fountain, bent down on his knees, brought out a small case from his pocket. Louise was all stunned by his act, her mouth opened in shock. He opened the case, and it had a beautiful white gold ring that had the letter "L" written on it since they both shared the same initials in their names.

"I Love you", Lucian announced.

"Me too", Louise had replied with all her emotions.

Who would have thought that the new couple, met in a cocktail bar, would form a real-life relationship? A year went by in the lives of Louise and Lucian, and they still had very young love. When they were together, they would have the feeling as cheerful, as a teenager would embrace. He trusted her with his life. Lucian was comfortable enough to open up and tell her about his experiences; including many memories about his past life that he was unable to talk to anyone else but Louise. Louise also came to know that he had a reputation for being known as the bad boy.

THE PAST

Before meeting Lucian, Louise had a history of issues going in her life. In the space of a year after her marriage breakup, she had slept with around 60 different men! She had a bad reputation as a whore. Louise had a vague idea about her being a notorious bitch, but her mental condition did not stop her. Louise had gone in such a depressed state that she had no respect for herself, no morals. How was it possible to be given deference by others if Louise did not have it for herself? No extra effort was required from others since she gave herself freely away.

She would feel high for many days, no sleep, lack of appetite, resilient and intense interests into something such as a new hobby. Alternatively, she would like to go after an item she wanted to buy. Louise would speak faster than usual and had a sense of euphoria. She would become very hyperactive and had very little concentration for anything. After 4 days of no sleep and lots of physical and mental activity, her temper would change to feeling extremely tired, no motivation. Her moods had severe swings. The interests she had for any hobby or items would have vanished in no time.

She would spend many days or weeks in bed.

Her behaviour was at an extreme level. She would only have to see something once, such as an advert about baking cakes, and she had this overwhelming, keen interest in trying to start learning to bake. For some time, gardening was her craze too, where she spent almost two months buying various types of plants and gardening tools. After some time, she would lose interest in gardening before moving onto the next hobby. Thinking back to her attention throughout the lifetime, if adequately, had around over 40 different hobbies. She kept changing those after a particular spell of higher enthusiasm. The worst thing about her hobbies was that after losing interest, she never wanted to look back at those. Once she moved to the next hobby, the previous had no place in her life.

Lucian, on the other hand, had a bad past too.

Growing into his teens, Lucian sadly lost his mum to a sudden stroke. This tore his heart, he stood above her, not knowing why she was on the floor, not moving, and he had strange, unpleasant, heart-breaking feelings inside him that he did not know how to deal with it or to react. Years after his mother's death, Lucian never cried, never appropriately grieved for her. He had eventually just felt anger, pain, and hate but never knew why. He started to go out with friends, stealing, taking people's money, and drinking alcohol on a daily basis.

The character he was beginning to become was not really who he was. He struggled to express or show any genuine emotions that he was really feeling. He would steal from people's homes, drive illegally, and soon became a gang member. He had a lot of female attention and had multiple sexual relationships, but never had any connection or feelings towards them. It was his way; of being able to deal and manage his own grief of losing his mum some years before—mother and son bond. Born in Russia with his family, in an inferior home, the boy had a great relationship with his mum.

He always used to sleep snuggled up close to her in bed and would find comfort holding on to her breast all night one he was a toddler. This was a comfort zone for him but eventually had to stop this because he got older and was not acceptable. His mum was a gorgeous slim woman with long dark hair and big bright brown eyes. She always cared for him and made sure that he got the best in life, although they were poor. He would most of the time, go out stealing food to take home for the family to be fed. He felt like he had a responsibility to look after his family. He loved his mum with all his heart, and losing her was a change to heave life—bad boy.

The boy reached his adulthood. He was in his early twenties and had an interest in the nightlife, females, prostitutes and alcohol. His life was real money-orientated because he had been through the hard times in his life due to lack of funds. Money was everything in his life because you could buy nothing without payment, and no happiness was there in being poor. His views on life were just about happiness from money and party. He had those negative thoughts when you want to snatch something that is not readily available in your life. Most evenings, the boy will meet with friends at the local pub to have drinks together with many alcoholic shots, Jack Daniels and beers. He would always manage to get a girl's attention. He had a charm for females, a tall, and dark-haired slim built but with stiff muscles, smells of fresh spice perfume and had a lovely smile. Calling him a snake charmer would not be wrong.

When Louise met Lucian, they built a magical connection between them that helped them to change each other for good. Lucian changed her so much; He showed what love is and how real it can be. Before he came along, she was empty, alone, lost, and confused. Louise had forgotten who she was and what she wanted in life, but then Lucian came together and made her smile again. He gave her extreme feelings inside, which she never knew existed.

Likewise, Louise changed Lucian's perspective on money and happiness. To her, joy and love were much above the money or material. She gave him her pure love, time, and attention. They both made a beautiful couple, which was admired by people around them.

THE CELEBRATION

One week before the New Year's eve 2019, Lucian was at work in the car wash with his friends, Andrei and Mo. The same two people Louise met on the first night she met Lucian. All from Russia, they worked together with him. Lucian had known them for some years. Louise had her first contact with Andrei and Mo when she first met her partner Lucian in summer 2017. Another person by the name of Emil, he was from Hungary, had only just started working with Lucian recently.

Both Louise and Lucian would either go to visit Andrei for drinks at his home, which happened to just be a room he rented. It was a shared house with other people living there. It was only a small square room with just a tiny table next to his single bed and one wardrobe full of clothes. They never attended Mo's place where he stayed. Still, Mo would sometimes come with Andrei to their home whenever Louise invited her boyfriend's friends over to have parties or if it was a special occasion.

They were all good friends and trusted each other to a certain extent. Andrei would always call Louise "his sister," but sometimes went too far and annoyed Lucian. He could be too touchy towards her, continually pulling at her hand to kiss the back of it but in a friendly manner. Louise was OK as she is the kind of person who just likes to get along with others and is a very outgoing person.

Mo was easily led into things. He was scruffy and believed to be a virgin. People would try to take advantage of him and steal from him his money if he had any. He also liked gambling together with Andrei in the local betting shops. They often spent a lot of time together after finishing work. Sometimes Lucian would join them too but not often. Louise spoke highly of Mo. She would protect him from others as he was always at the receiving end of harm. She never liked to hear about him being hurt.

One week before New Year's Eve, Louise and Lucian decided to arrange a New Year's Eve party at their home and invited the three lads to come over. They were pleased to be asked. Very excitedly, everyone made plans for that evening. They went over many times to decide what drinks to bring. Lucian's friends were very excited and discussed what time to come there and so on.

New Year's Eve arrived; Lucian and Louise went to the town shopping centre to buy what they needed for the evening. They got two crates of beers, two bottles of wine, shots, Vodka, and some frozen food to cook before their friends arrived. Excited for the evening, both Louise and Lucian got themselves ready and gathered what to wear. Louise decided to put on her favourite dress, red lace, knee length tight dress with black heels and a vanilla perfume. Lucian wore his black suit and white shirt.

At 8 pm sharp, a black Audi arrived outside the front door; it was Mo, Andrei, and Emil. They were using their boss's car. The doorbell rang, and Louise walked, wearing her high heels, making clicking sounds on the wood flooring as she opened the front door. Lucian was coming down the stairs at the same time to invite them all into the house. Mo walked in first, looking cute and smart in Jeans and a t-shirt. Andrei came in after; he smelled of fresh aftershave and looked clean and tidy. He was dressed in blue jeans and a red-buttoned shirt. The Russian shook Lucian's hand and kissed Louise on the cheek excitedly.

"Hello, my sister", He giggled.

Emil was behind Andrei and shook Lucian's hand.

"Hello", He said to Louise.

She then closed the door after them all. They walked together behind one another down the hall into the front room. It was a pleasant, courteous walk in a single file. The party had started, and it was noisy. Everyone was excited and choosing which drink they wanted to begin with. Louise had already prepared a glass of champagne before they had arrived. That was their first drink to celebrate.

"Cheers", all shouted as they tapped each other's glasses against each other.

Music was played at a smooth volume level in the living room, which was just down the hallway from the front door. The kitchen was opposite to the front. In the living room on the right, as you walked in, there was a three-seater sofa facing the TV, which was the main attraction of the living room. Just opposite the couch, there was a small armchair facing the hall. Right in the middle of the room was a 6 Ft. pool table ready for playing later. There was a dartboard just above the armchair on the wall.

The roulette game was left placed on top of a sizable white unit to the left of the living room wall. This game was based on filling each shot glass with Alcohol. In turn, someone would spin the wheel with a small metal ball on top. Whichever number the ball landed on, the person would have to take the shot glass with the matching name on it and colour then quickly pour it down the throat.

On New Year's Eve, Louise prepared for the evening to celebrate the special occasion with their mutual friends. Mo, Andrei, and Emil. She wore a stunning, red knee-length lace dress, and her partner was wearing a nice handsome black suit. She had drinks prepared and a small food buffet on the table. She also stood aside from the pool table, and the "Shot Roulette Game" was on the side. She was all ready to play games and have fun. You use this game to consume Alcohol—a lot of it.

What is Shot Roulette?

The game features a roulette wheel with several shot glasses around the edge of the wheel. Each of these glasses will have two numbers on them, which will correspond to the numbers on the wheel. There are no set game rules in shot roulette.

The evening started with playing music from Louise's mobile phone on YouTube application. She had her cell phone connected to the stereo by Bluetooth. Lucian made sure everybody was happy and had his or her drinks filled, and kept his friends entertained.

Sometime later, everybody had a few more drinks, Andrei started walking around the living room, laughing and joking. The boys would often go outside in the garden for a cigarette. The garden patio doors were to the side of the small armchair at the back of the living room. As you went out the doors, there was hard wooden decking painted black, and it was creaky.

To the right of the garden on the decking was a small spa with some artificial trees placed around it. Straight ahead, there was a fabricated brick BBQ. Louise kept asking if they wanted refills or if they were hungry. Everyone was enjoying himself and celebrating the evening with a mixture of Russian songs, English party tunes, and Reggae. It was all fun and games.

Mo was the quietest among all boys, partially because he knew very little English, a few words only. He was already drunk when he arrived. He was crouched up on the sofa many times and even fell asleep for a while at one point.

The people were all gathered together, talking and laughing, and Louise was singing along and watching the lads enjoying themselves. Then, she saw Andrei quickly and excitedly walking happily towards her as she was sitting down on the sofa. He leaned down, facing towards her, and placed his right hand onto the phone screen to turn over the music. In one quick moment, Andrei started to slowly touch her by sneakily rubbing his right arm against Louise's leg gently and a little too long for her comfort. He then tapped her leg with the back of his hand as he moved away. He then got up and walked away back to where the other lads were all standing next to the roulette game on the table against the wall.

Louise was feeling confused but ignored his action because she was a little shaken up to believe Andrei would do such a thing. Especially in the home of his best friend, and that too, with his friend's love of life.

She decided to go and tell her partner about what happened and how much she felt uncomfortable. After listening to her, Lucian was furious. Louise could see it in his eyes and how he kept questioning her for more details. They both agreed after some time speaking to each other, not to make a drama out of it. Lucian started watching Andrei closely, while she got Lucian's phone to record any further inappropriate behaviours for evidence on their side if anything happened.

THE SURVEILLANCE

She prepared the mobile phone and started recording, facing the camera towards where she would be sitting most of the evening. As a precautionary measure, she had arranged to perform surveillance if anything more were to happen to her from Andrei. It would be recorded without him knowing because she hid the camera well, it was at a distance, and no one could see it.

Most of the evening, everyone kept going in-and-out of the living room. Louise had spent most of her time sitting on the sofa in the middle of the camera's view. They both had forgotten at some point that the phone was there on record. They had just carried on with the evening to try to enjoy them.

Andrei did not touch her anymore for some time after they started the recording. There were many jokes about Andrei and Emil; they spent a lot of the night talking to each other outside the living room. Emil was Hungarian, but he could speak good English and a little Russian. Andrei was Russian, and he could be fluent in English. Still, he was mixing both Russian and English together sometimes when he was laughing about Emil. Louise could not quite understand exactly what they were joking about.

It was awkward for her, but the fact that her boyfriend knew the language comforted her. Lucian would stop his friends if they were winding her up. She trusted her partner. However, the East Europeans would still have a conversation with her in English so she could understand and laugh about it. They did not want her to think anything was out of place in their jokes.

Together, they all played a game of pool a couple of times, then later they played Shot Roulette. Some drinks were spilt over on the floor, one by Andrei and another time by Mo. Lucian cleaned up the mess that Andrei had just spilt over while playing shot roulette. Louise saw from a distance that Andrei had taken his turn with the shot roulette to spin, and she noticed Andrei's right arm swung out too far aside him and hit the glass over.

It was turning out to be weird!

At one point, Louise went to the kitchen. Mo followed her to the kitchen; she had traced his footsteps to be following her. Louise tried to act normal and continued to walk towards the fridge. As she opened the refrigerator door, she started to feel a little uncomfortable because Mo got a little too close than usual. Since Louise trusted him as a good friend, she did not think much more of it.

Later in the evening, Andrei walked towards Louise as she was sitting on the sofa, kneeling down; he changed over the current music playing on her phone again. He then started rubbing his elbow against her leg and tapped his backhand on the same leg as she moved away. At this time, Louise had it in her mind about the phone she had hidden and knew what Andrei has just done, is now recorded. She knew it could be used as concrete evidence. Louise was able to show Lucian what his best friend really is like!

A few minutes later, Louise was in the kitchen, refilling some drinks for the guests. Afterwards, she walked back towards the front room, down the hallway. As she was entering the front area, she saw the boys walk in from the garden to notice Andrei had his trousers undone. He was just pulling them up, fixing his belt together. Louise asked him what he was doing, and he replied that he had peed in the garden. She believed him and continued the rest of the evening, as usual. The poor girl was enjoying the music, singing, dancing, and joining the Shot Roulette, without realising what was going on.

Not a care in the world.

They were all in the living room. Mo was standing up, and Emil was sitting on the front. Opposite them, both Louise and Lucian were seated on the three-seater, the main attraction of the lounge. Lucian was on the right side of Louise on the sofa, and Andrei was on her left. Lucian was sitting just forward, leaning on the edge of the couch, busy speaking to Emil. Louise's partner had no idea about the evil intentions of his friends.

Andrei then suddenly picked up Louise's phone that she had left earlier, on the arm of the sofa. He then moved the cell phone towards her. Andrei placed it directly onto her lap; he slid his hand slowly, sexually, and for longer than usual to accept it to be appropriate.

Louise had reacted nervously and gently elbowed his arm in an attempt to show Andrei it was not wanted. He ignored her entirely and continued to do what he was doing with her phone. Louise did not ask for her cell phone at all, to be passed to her; this was random.

How is she going to explain this to her partner? Again, he had touched her without consent. He had betrayed his best friend, Lucian.

Andrei had spent much of his time getting close to Louise. Time after time, he was going over to her to change the music and getting too close on purpose. *Those were all excuses.* He was leaning over her at one point to speak to Mo, although it was possible to talk to his friend from where he was standing. Andrei had insisted on photos to be captured of just Louise and him together, with his phone and no one else to be in the picture. Lucian was a little uncomfortable about this but agreed to keep the peace.

A few hours went by, and Louise found herself alone, in the living room with Andrei, while the rest of the boys were in the garden. They were just chatting and having a cigarette. Her boyfriend showed them the garden, and the finished work of building the BBQ place.

Andrei was sitting on the sofa, leaning backwards and relaxing opposite her. She was in the armchair at the time, and he started to speak about something, which was quite alarming to her. He told her that she should change her dress.

"Why"? She asked him.

"Because you are too sexy in that dress"! Andrei responded with a cheap line.

As he said this, he sat up, moved forward to the edge of the seat. He looked down at the certain gesture he was making with his lower body. He started spreading both of his Legs outward.

"Maybe somebody will look up there," He said with a snarky look on his face, smiling.

Louise instantly became uncomfortable and surprised that he would say something like this. He then told her she should message him some time without Lucian knowing!

How dare he betray his friend like this?

Louise slightly ignored this and picked up her phone that was on her lap, and she started to type away. She did not know precisely what she was trying to do on her phone; she was nervous and obnoxious about Andrei.

In one moment very quickly, the girl had this sense that someone was next to her. Louise instantly looked up to see Andrei's lips in the front view of her eyes. He was very close to her face. She had the impression that he was trying to kiss her. Therefore, she stood up very quickly, raised her right arm out to his chest, and pushed him away forcefully. She told him very calmly, but clearly that this girl is not interested. Louise repeated the fact that she was in love with Lucian. He should respect his friend for having him in our home.

"You should not be doing this," Louise announced with firm intent in her tone, though she was scared to death inside. This cold response made Andrei agree. He quickly said sorry, and then he sat down back to where he was.

About 5 minutes later, Lucian and the other two boys walked back inside into the front room. Lucian went straight into the kitchen. Louise followed him, agitated, very nervous, and shaky. She stressed with emotions, the sound of her words and tone were trembling, and she struggled to get words out to tell him not to leave her alone with his friends, ever again. Louise quickly rushed upstairs, very distressed, and went into her bedroom. She was looking in her wardrobe, something that would cover her up. Wearing jeans and a T-shirt, she headed back downstairs. Her boyfriend asked her what was wrong because he could see her being very nervous and clumsy. In time, after she calmed down, she told him precisely what Andrei had said, and he tried to kiss her while everybody was out in the garden.

Now, it was Lucian's turn to be very nervous and angry. He wanted to speak to Andrei in that very instance. Still, Louise begged him not to do anything because Lucian could lose control. And if he lost his temper, he could be in trouble if he was to hit Andrei. Moreover, Andrei would deny it. Lucian could become furious quickly and fight without thinking. Besides, she did not want to cause a scene or have trouble. Louise was a quiet person; she really did not like violence at all. Her boyfriend agreed that he would not say anything and would talk to his friend once they left; also, both of them knew they had the phone on the recording. So, they would look through the video later once the boys had all gone. They tried to be calm and continue as usual.

The boys all went together in the garden AGAIN, and Andrei kept asking Lucian, "Have I done something wrong""

"I am so sorry." Andrei kept repeating this and kept on acting nervous.

Maybe Andrei thought she had told Lucian what he did. Louise noticed Andrei had gone very quiet and did not pay her any more attention whatsoever.

Something had changed.

Did he hear Louise tell Lucian in the kitchen? Because they both did not mention anything to him about what he had done to Louise. She did not see much of her boyfriend, Lucian, that evening. Maybe because there was too much going on. She does have awful conditions and possibly bipolar. Moreover, she quickly forgets things or gets overexcited easily, which makes her distracted quickly.

Lucian is not the one who forgets easily; he remembers so many things and never struggles with his memory. The evening ended very suddenly. Andrei was the first to decide to leave.

"I am Tired" He excused.

The boys stayed until around five in the morning. Andrei and Emil left together, although Emil did not want to go yet. Later, Mo left on his own in a taxi.

THE REVEAL

L ucian and Louise started to tidy up the mess that everyone had left behind. Apart from what happened with Andrei, they both spoke about having enjoyed the night.

They both later sat down together and recalled the recording that Louise had started hours earlier. Watching the video together, not only had they caught Andrei touching Louise's leg at that time, but more. They were shocked in disbelief of what they found out.

They saw precisely when Andrei had rubbed his arm against her leg and tapped with his backhand. This was awful for Lucian to see it with his own eyes. He was so possessive about his girlfriend, now he was seeing his friend touching her inappropriately. He felt terrible for Louise.

After he had closely watched the video, he asked her why she was winking at Andrei. *At one point in the video, Louise had blinked her eye in the direction where Andrei was sitting, which was a Motor Tic.* She tried explaining to him that I was not winking; it was an involuntary tic. It made her unable to control some movements and even more so when she had been drinking Alcohol. Later, after some time of arguing over this, he understood her condition. Lucian was nervous about this. He started to look more into the video to then see that Andrei had his phone facing the screen towards his girlfriend more often than an accepted norm, throughout the recording. The video was only 2 hours long because it had died of battery.

They watched again more closely, from the beginning of the video towards the very end. Both significant others put so much attention to every single split second, every solo minute and every minor detail. It only led to then finding out, there was more to it. Something was fishy, and it caught their eye. More things were going on without them knowing.

That time, when Louise walked towards the boys, coming in from the garden, she asked Andrei what he was doing with his trousers. Andrei had not peed while he was in the garden. That guy was actually pulling his pants down and undone them as he was walking into the front room!

How strange, for a man to do this random bizarre act. Still, he managed to make it believable that he went to take a piss. It is a little disrespectful to even do that, let alone flash his underwear in front of a woman in her home!

Looking more in-depth into the video, Mo was sitting on one chair, which was not far from the Christmas tree. *They had set up a beautiful Christmas tree 15 days before the New Year's.* Louise and Lucian noticed that his leg was to his far left. He was acting quite suspicious, moving very slow with his legs. It looked like he was trying to reach out for something. Watching closely, they continued to monitor this behaviour zoomed in the video. He intended to drop his phone from his hands, and it landed in between his feet. They heard the sound of the drop from his phone. Mo then leaned over to reach out, but he did not bend downwards in between his feet for his phone, he was reaching out to where his foot was reaching out beforehand - on his far-left Next to the Christmas tree.

Then they saw him picking up a different mobile phone. Now, this rang all kinds of alarms and concerns for both of them. They had many questions. Whose phone was that? Why does Mo have two phones? Why did Mo take the time to pick it up? Things did not add up.

Not long after Mo had picked up the phone, he passed it to Andrei. Clearly, he had picked up Andrei's phone. Now at this point, she and her boyfriend were incredibly nervous. Both shaking, angry, and feeling betrayed. Surely, there was more than they knew. Louise's heart was racing, she could not believe what she was seeing, yet she and Lucian never noticed anything during the gathering. How could they miss that?

Hours and hours, they both spent, looking over the video recording of that evening. There was more to come! By now, they were shocked, sceptical, and feeling mixed emotions. Both were shaking and having many thoughts going through their minds.

Nervously, they continued to watch the video, pausing and rewinding so many times. They noticed that, not long after Andrei had done the part with his Jeans earlier, Mo was acting strangely in one corner of the front room.

Studying very carefully, the video showed Louise was out of the room and soon had come back in from the hallway. As she was walking towards the pool table, Mo had his Jeans undone and opened. He walked past her precisely at that time as she had walked in! He planned this. He waited for her to step in and then to walk past her, flashing himself as he did. Again, she did not notice it when it happened in real-time. She was oblivious to it all that evening. How could they not see what was going on?

Louise felt sick at that moment, watching this on the phone now and having no idea of it happening at the time. She felt the ground open up. Not only did Andrei open up his trousers, but also did Mo, later on! *How disrespectful to do this in front of a woman in her home.*

Lucian was Russian and spoke perfect English. The video had audio too, so they could listen to conversations. As they were speaking in Russian mostly, Louise could not understand a word they were saying. However, Lucian listened carefully and re-played those dialogues over and over the video. Some were clear and able to understand, and some were muffled, or music had taken over the voices.

More of the video was listened to, and Lucian had put all the conversation together. He was sickened to his brain. Most of the communication between Andrei and Emil was about his lover, Louise. They were speaking in code words to each other, so Louise and Lucian did not understand.

Everything that was spoken was sexual and obsessively about her. Andrei said to Emil, "I want the red" repeatedly while playing pool. Now you would think that it is normal he is playing pool and wanted the red coloured ball.

Well, during the roulette game, Andrei again said, "I want the red" a couple of times to Emil. Remember Louise was wearing red that evening. He would repeatedly speak about taking a woman home, do this, and do that. He also mentioned an erotic idea he had

"I put this ball in her a**", He said.

Emil spent most of the evening telling Andrei to stop and be quiet. While Lucian and Louise were in the garden together, Andrei said extremely nervously to Emil, "Lucian's not drunk",

"There's more to come, don't worry", Emil replied.

What was their plan? Why was Andrei so nervous that he is not drunk? Both Louise and Lucian began to believe they both were trying to get Lucian drunk and hope he is to pass out or something serious anyway.

If this plan worked, what was their plan next?

At the table where the Roulette was, Andrei, Lucian, and Emil were taking turns to spin the wheel. It was Andrei's turn; as he spun the wheel, he had knocked over a bottle of beer. Watching the video more closely, Louise noticed that Andrei had intended to do this to distract Lucian. Lucian began to clean the spillage up from the floor with a cloth that was nearby. At that time, Andrei made his way towards Louise. He was staggering side to side, looking silly and giggly when making his way to the sofa. As Andrei went to lean down facing her, Emil sprinted behind him, very nervously. He grabbed Andrei up to force him calmly and discreetly to take him outside in the garden to talk. Andrei tried to resist, but gave up and walked with Emil out. The recording showed that they were outside together for around 15 minutes.

They reached at the point during the recording where Mo was suspiciously playing about with his blue puffer jacket. He had placed the jumper on his lap sitting on the sofa next to Louise on her left side. Louise and Lucian questioned each other about what the heck Mo was doing. Mo kept at it for so long, almost 15 minutes; they could not figure it out even after repeatedly observing.

Why did Emil take Andrei out? What was going on? Did Emil know what was going on? Was he involved? As Emil and Andrei walked back inside, Lucian noticed in the video of Andrei's shadow on one wall showing the shadow leaning downwards and leaning under the Christmas tree. Andrei placed the phone there!

As for Mo's behaviour, this all came as a shock to them both.

They believed he would never have the mental capability to do something with such sharp moves. They always looked at him as a gentleman. He could not hurt anyone; it was impossible, or so they perceived. He never had a proper relationship with a girl, and his friends would tease him about being a virgin. Louise saw him as a softy, and if she were to see people try to take advantage of him, she would be the first to speak out and stick up for him. There was no reason to not trust him before New Year's night.

Andrei would call Louise "his sister" all the time since he first met her. He called her the same during all that evening as well. Giving her regular high fives and would kiss her kindly on the cheek as a friend, which she was used to.

He would often seem desperate for a girl, be very quickly clingy to them, and nag them for their contact details. He had no morals at all. Although Andrei had this character, Louise never thought he would betray his friends.

Emil had only been to their home one time before New Year's evening. Both Louise and Lucian did not know him very well, but he seemed friendly enough. Emil was married. His wife was due to have a baby soon. Louise and Lucian had no reason to be cautious of him.

Never would they both have thought that these people would have the mentality to do what they did in such a professional way. Louise and Lucian were totally unaware and oblivious to feel about them as innocent. They managed to secretly hide their phones, speak in code to each other, and flash their underwear without the hosts knowing and more!

They must have planned it all out before they arrived that New Year's evening. Maybe they had done this before, and they knew all about it. Possibly, done similar to someone else! Watching more of the recording, they noticed Andrei had his phone on him always. Especially when he was near Louise! Aiming often towards Louise's chest and legs.

He had intended to drop money on the floor facing her when she sat on the sofa. He then bent down to pick it up, with the phone in the same hand aiming towards her. They could see his screen because the video recorder was placed behind him, so he was back towards the camera of Lucian's phone. Andrei's phone at the back was the camera facing towards Louise on the sofa, and the screen showed a specific website for a live broadcast. Louise and Lucian could not figure out which website it was, although it was visible on the recording. It was LIVE.

This made them both believe that Louise had secretly been recorded most of the night, Live on a broadcasting website! This website was also known to earn money. They were making money from the benefit of highlighting Louise. Watching more into the video, they also saw that Mo was fiddling about too long with his jacket placed on his lap. He was doing it while sitting next to Louise. After more attention and watching closely, they noticed under Mo's jacket was his mobile phone, he was aiming it to capture Louise's legs! He was doing this very cleverly.

What a dirty, sneaky pervert, Louise thought.

How had this all happened without them knowing? Didn't Lucian listen to their conversations about her? Was he involved? She had so many questions and thoughts in her head. Her body had been exposed without her knowledge and placed on some application, and God knows where else.

What were these people's intentions? What was the plan? *They were earning money from the benefit of displaying Louise.* She started searching for the logo of the website, which showed live broadcast on New Year's Eve, it was a private website. The particular website was limited only to members. The landing web page highlighted the fact that the members buy and sell women. **They were broadcasting her Live for the buyers.** It was an illegal sex trafficking website. Louise was entirely devastated because she was not only a victim of sexual assault but Sex Trafficking.

Of course, she started questioning her boyfriend, who she had accused at one point of being involved. She was stupid to think this because, if he was involved, then why he had let her record it in the first place. How did he translate word for word what the people spoke of her? She did not have proof that her boyfriend was involved, and she believed totally that he had no idea! Especially when Andrei had become nervous beforehand about Lucian not being drunk yet.

Were Andrei and Emil trying to spike Lucian's drink? Louise would not put it past them. After watching so many below the belt moves, anything could be expected.

After Lucian had heard all the conversations among everybody, he was sickened to have to explain it to Louise. His friends of all the people spoke nonstop of sexual content and what they wanted to do with her. This was torture for Lucian to hear such disgusting and abusive words that were about the love of his life that he adored dearly and protects. They were both still shocked by how they never clicked on to anything. They even heard Emil and Andrei talking about Louise, where Andrei used the words "I fuck her for 5 pounds". Maybe they did manage to put drugs in not only Lucian's drink but maybe in hers too!

Louise just wanted to die; she had been humiliated. So many emotions that were impossible to explain and feeling confused, and she did not know what reality was anymore. The anger she felt was something she had never felt before, she was not the same at all. There are no words to describe her feelings. She felt exposed to the whole world, without her Consent, which ran a chill down her spine.

THE INVESTIGATIONS

L ucian was in so much anger and despair. His friends, who he believed he could trust, had just violated the love of his life! How was he ever going to forgive or even forget what they had done?

Lucian asked Louise to tell the Police ASAP, Louise agreed, and they reported what happened to the local authorities. Louise was scared about this because firstly, how was she going to explain this as it was unimaginable. Moreover, what were those accused people going to do if they knew Louise reported them, will they be in revenge to hurt her? This was a complicated situation for her.

When two police officers arrived, Louise asked them to come into the front room because it would be easier for her to explain the situation of what happened. The officers asked many questions, and Louise explained that she has the recording of it all. She then pulled out her phone and played a short clip of when Andrei had touched her leg, passing the phone to her lap. Also, a different video clip of when he had his cell phone aimed towards her up the dress. It was when he bent down to the floor, that time to pick up the money he had dropped intentionally.

She was advised to transfer the recordings from her phone onto a memory stick for the officer to be able to use. So, the department can watch it on a computer in the station. They both sat together on their son's computer later that evening, loading the videos from the phone onto the computer. Having to look at the videos again and now on a bigger screen. They also thought it would be better if they just edited the Footage into parts that show straight to the incidents to help the Police see what they needed to watch.

Going through the videos again, Louise felt sick to her stomach. While trying to remember that night, they were all together; she still could not explain why she had not seen anything at the very moment.

"I'm sorry, I let you down". Lucian apologised to her.

"I should have protected you from all this". Lucian further added.

"I didn't even take attention to their conversation, I don't remember much of the night either," Lucian explained.

"It is okay, was not your fault", Louise knew he had no control or power to do anything because he did not know.

One early afternoon, a week later, the police officer arrived at Louise's home in her police car to take her to the station to make her statement. It was a cold winter's day. Louise was in the back of the police car, quiet all the way through the journey. The officer was reassuring her that everything was ok. They drove up to the end of the police station, and many other police cars were parked up alongside each other. It was tranquil as they got out of the vehicle.

The officer led Louise through some double doors, walking down the corridor; the building had small, white walls and echo. They entered into a small office, with two chairs and a desk with a computer screen on top, papers, and a pen. Louise was being questioned about what happened on the night of 31st December. She had to recall all that happened. Louise struggled to think clearly. She explained she could only remember a little because of the trauma from knowing what she saw in the video. The officer was very understanding and calm.

She had the memory stick with her and gave it to the police officer in charge. Also, she handed over the saved videos on a memory stick. The Police received Louise's full statement at the station. Plus, they took the Footage that was recorded onto a memory stick to use for evidence later on if needed. She wrote every word Louise said, on the computer, then printed it out and gave it to her to sign.

It took a while for the officer to look and investigate what she had complained about so far. She told them, this was a case for Sexual assault and possibly for Upskirting. However, the Police found it difficult to establish the alleged crime based on the video she could provide.

"Difficult to prove Upskirting? How, when it is on video? 3

times or more, he is aiming his phone upwards into Louise's dress", She thought to herself but felt helpless.

"Dropping items intentionally, to bend over and aiming the phone upwards near Louise, How can this not be enough evidence"? Louise was slightly aggrieved.

It was evident in the video, Andrei touched her leg inappropriately, and this is what they should point more on for a Charge.

Andrei was unable to contact, he apparently left his job and moved home. Police kept searching for him. Soon after they tried to contact him, they put him on the wanted list on their system.

Five months later and no luck finding him, the police officer had new information about a new address where he lived. That address was attended to. One of the tenants that lived there answered the door. The officer asked him if Andrei was inside. The tenant confirmed he knew of him, but Andrei did not live there anymore. The officer then stressed to the person standing at the door that Andrei was on their wanted system and that the alleged offender was to contact the office the next day. The person said he would contact Andrei to give him the information.

The next day after this, Andrei handed himself over to the police station.

Lucian could no longer attend work anymore. How could he

work with these people at the same job? This had affected both of them together.

They only managed to record two hours, but what else happened that they did not know about?

Louise began to believe that she was recorded in the bathroom, why not, when they documented everything else. What did they do with these videos and possible photos of her? She might never know.

Louise and Lucian watched the recording repeatedly for days, rewinding back, pausing, and zooming in the video. They kept listening to every single word spoken to each other and focused their minds on that video for days nonstop. They did not sleep; they were not tired, maybe because of the shock.

Trying to recall that night when all of them were together, drinking and celebrating the evening. They both realised that they did not remember anything other than what they had watched repeatedly. It is as if their brains were switched off for that evening. The video footage had become their reality because they had put so much into watching the recording. *The Footage had taken over reality.*

Strange how they now have memories of these actions and awful behaviours stuck in their minds but were **Impervious** to the danger!

This event had put a significant impact on Louise. She started to become paranoid to the point of believing they were watching her all the time when she was home alone or out shopping. This woman would keep having to look behind her because she would feel uncomfortable and in danger of something. She would think that Andrei, Mo, and Emil were following her moves.

THE VOICES

Her privacy had been taken from her. Before the shower, she would feel the need to check the room for hidden cameras or phones. Looking under household items, behind the sink and toilet. At night, she would have to check often that the windows and doors are locked before going to bed.

As Louise was lying in bed to go to sleep, she could not close her eyes. She would have great difficulty feeling safe when closing her eyes. She got an enormous, intense fear rushing through her body. And images appeared in her mind that someone was coming in the house to harm her. Her brain would keep on waking her up that there was an intruder.

She took hours to finally sleep after watching around the bedroom and getting up many times to look out the window and down the stairway. If she did not check, then she remained in fear, her heart started racing, and the mind had visions of someone there in the home. Her conditions had worsened again, full throttle. She developed anxiety, and the extreme behaviour made a comeback because of Andrei, Mo, and Emil!

The police outcome.

Lucian and Louise were sitting together on a gorgeous, soft-sanded beach, watching the waves of the sea and feeling relaxed on a hot summer day, Louise's phone rang. She leaned to her side, reached out for her bag, and grabbed the phone. The screen showed the officer in charge of the case.

"Hello", Very nervously, Louise answered.

"Hello Louise, it's PC Smith, I have got information from the sergeant, and I'm afraid it is bad news", PC Smith said in a professional tone.

PC Smith was the Police officer in charge of the investigation.

Louise knew instantly what it was going to be. She listened to the officer speaking more while she was shaking nervously. She held the phone to her ear. Lucian was leaning up close to her phone to listen to the conversation.

"There isn't enough evidence for the court to go ahead and charge Andrei or Mo". Police officer states *in a professional tone.*

After 8 months of investigations, the couple had hoped the criminals were going to pay for what they had done. The Police outcome came negative. Louise wanted to get justice; the news was given to her. The case was dismissed!

"What? No!" She shouted in horror.

"How"? Louise asked the Police officer. In anger and disbelief, she had replied aggressively.

"But I have everything on tape", Louise had increased her pitch more than she would usually like.

"How is this not enough, what more do you want, to actually see him on top of me"? She questioned.

"You even said you saw it all yourself in the video of the touching," Louise exclaimed.

"The video isn't enough evidence to go ahead with the CPS, and the case will be dropped". The officer told her.

Louise was fuming, she could not accept the results, crying, shaking, and let down by the Police. She demanded them to look again into the case more, but they could not. Andrei, Mo, and Emil were free to walk away, laughing at Louise to their friends. She felt no one believed her. *The Voices started whispering to her.*

THE SELF DEFENCE

Tom lived with his mother, Louise, for the weekdays. He would visit his father on weekends. Her mum's boyfriend, Lucian, loved and provided for Tom more than his biological father. Louise had developed a perfect homely environment for her son, with the help of her partner. Tom would anxiously wait for Lucian to come home. He always called his mother's partner by his name, Lucian. Tom looked up to him, the way he cared for his mum. They had established an extraordinary family bond. Lucian's birthday arrived, and it was a hot summer weekend. Tom had decided to stay home to honour his mum's boyfriend instead of visiting his biological father. Lucian planned to take Louise out for dinner, to the new restaurant, called Merlin that had recently opened in their town. It was only a five-minute drive away. Tom refused to go with them because he wanted to give them some personal space on their special day.

Louise and Lucian were very excited to celebrate his special day. Both dressed very elegantly and sophisticatedly. Louise was wearing a slim black dress, with shiny black heels. She also had her black glitter clutch bag that was her Christmas gift from Lucian. 8:00 pm and the couple was ready to leave the house. Louise used her phone to call a taxi to take them to the location of the restaurant. The cab did not take very long and arrived within 10 minutes.

They both sat at the back of the taxi together and told the driver where they wanted to go. 5 minutes after the journey, they arrived at the restaurant. It was very well presented. The ambience was attractive. Many huge windows were showing the inside and had beautiful lights shining outside with lovely trees on either side of the entrance door. Laid out at the entrance, was a gorgeous, red rug leading towards the central area.

Lucian paid the taxi fare, opened his side of the door, and helped lead Louise safely out of the car. It was all part of the routine for him now. Holding her hand gently, just like a sober man. Holding hands together, they both walked side-by-side on the red, clean rug, *leading towards the entrance*. Above the entry door, there was a beautiful neon of the restaurant named Merlin.

One of the waiters opened the door to escort them to their booked space. The table looked very well presented, with crystal white fabric tablecloths. Crystal champagne glasses were placed neatly on the table, and the menus placed in the middle with a clear vase of flowers on the side.

Louise looked at the inside floor of the restaurant; it was polished Marble with a beautiful cream colour. Straight opposite to the entrance, was a long, marble top, lit bar with Cocktails and a display of wine bottles showing the background. It had a fresh feel to the room and many lovely lights on the edge of the bar. All the waiters were in tuxedos and very presentable with excellent manners. Just as Louise and Lucian were to be seated at their table, Louise noticed Emil with his wife and newborn baby, sitting on the table next to them.

Louise was OK, felt comfortable with this because there was no conflict between them, and had no problem with Emil about the New Year's Eve "celebration". Louise pinched Lucian on the arm and pointed out to make him aware that Emil was there. They acknowledged each other and said hello in a friendly tone.

After being seated at the table and looking through the menus together, Lucian and Emil started having a friendly conversation. They started catching up with how they both are and what they have been up to. Lucian continued to explain that they are both out together for his birthday. They intended to spend the rest of the evening in the Merlin restaurant to watch the live entertainment of the belly dancers.

Louise's son usually went away every weekend to his dad's house. Emil, Mo, and Andrei knew very well about the child being away on weekends because most of the time when they were at Louise and Lucian's home for drinks, it would be on the weekend. Therefore, they were very aware of the fact that the weekend is only with the couple at home. Louise and Emil's wife would be speaking between themselves; this was the first time they met. They discussed babies, fashion, and just about life in general.

A waiter came to take their order for food. Louise was not very hungry; she never had a good appetite. She ordered the mixed kebab selection with salad. Lucian ordered a large chicken grilled kebab, lettuce, and side chips.

For drinks, Lucian had a cider, and she had a glass of Rose. Emil soon excused himself to attend to the bathroom; he made a phone call to Mo.

He told Mo that Lucian is together with Louise in the same place as him, he went on to say to him that their home was empty. They were both aware that Louise left hard cash in the bedroom of her household. They made a quick plan that Mo will visit their house immediately, with a crowbar, and break into the front door quietly to not alert neighbours.

Emil offered half the cash to share with Mo if he agreed. 15 minutes later, the plan was agreed upon.

Emil's wife was feeding their baby with a bottle of baby milk. While waiting for Emil to come back to the table. Emil made his way back to his table next to Louise and Lucian's and created a new conversation about work and car washing. He did take some time in the men's toilets, but this was not something to question at the time.

9:30 pm Louise heard her phone ring, and she looked in her black glittery clutch bag that was placed on the table. She took out her mobile phone, and the screen showed the caller ID name as Tom. Her son.

Just as she answered the phone. Before she could say hello, she knew there was a problem. She could hear it in Tom's voice that there was something wrong. Tom sounded very frightened and nervous as he tried to alert her that there was some noise outside the front door and that he saw somebody walking around the house.

Tom's bedroom was the first room as you got to the top floor, landing to the right. His window faced the front of the house. He could see if anyone was at the front door. Tom was home alone. This weekend, he decided to stay home *because he wanted to spend the day with his mum for her boyfriend's birthday*. Tom was okay with him being at home alone that night, as it was for not long, presumably. It was planned that they would be home before 10pm. His anxiety meant he could not be alone for more extended periods. Tom also knew if there were any problems, then he could call her mother instantly. Louise had the cell phone on her at all times.

Louise tried to calm him down and asked him what was happening; Lucian immediately recognised Tom was in trouble by the way Louise was acting. He instantly called the Police and told the operator that someone was trying to get into the house. He stated to the Police that Tom was in there, all by himself. The emergency helpline operator asked for their home address, which Lucian provided.

Louise and Tom stayed on the phone together, listening to her frightened teen, scared for his life. Shaken up and not knowing what to do, Louise could only remain at the end of the phone and hope the Police arrived quickly. He was crying and extremely petrified.

Noises were coming from the front door downstairs, but not very loud. The sound of metal hitting together and cracking of wood was heard by Tom. He knew by this time that the door was broken open and heard footsteps on the floor tiles. A heavy metal sound made Tom jump in fear from his room, and he thought fast to protect himself. The intruder was now in the house; he could not see anything because it was dark, and Tom was in his bedroom upstairs. He had a single room of his own with just his computer table and one single bed next to a clothing unit.

Louise was telling Tom, they are on the way and insisted him to find something nearby, to grab, in case the person went for him. The situation was out of her control. All she could do was listen to the terror and fear that was transferring down the phone. Lucian stayed on the phone with the Police until they had arrived at their home. Emil's wife was a swift driver; she quickly drove them home to their son. Leaving Emil with the baby in the restaurant. Emil nervously called Mo, but there was no answer. He was not aware Tom was home.

Still on the phone together, Tom explained that the person was coming up the stairs. Someone he instantly recognised had suddenly approached him. As the man was about to grab him, Tom very quickly grabbed his right arm as he went to Tom's neck, he grabbed him with force. In one sudden quick action, Tom punched with full power to Mo's temple. Mo fell sideways, severely losing his balance and fell down the stairs hitting his head on the ground. Louise heard a Bang down the phone and a struggle. The phone suddenly went quiet.

Mo did not get up again. He had died of the fall.

She kept shouting down the phone, shaking uncontrollably. She repeated her son's name, many times over. "Tom, please answer. Where are you? What is happening? Are you OK? Tom, Answer me". She was going insane, thinking her son was harmed or even dead.

The Police arrived before Lucian and Louise. Louise started assisting the Police in trying to get into the home to make sure that her child was safe. Tom was escorted outside the house by a police officer, and he ran towards Louise, looking scared and lost. He cuddled her very tightly, uncontrollably. Louise and Lucian both grabbed him with all their might and comforted him. They were pleased to see him safe.

A few minutes later, an ambulance arrived, and the next thing Louise was told is that the intruder was announced dead at the scene. Louise asked her son if he knew of the person who was in the home, and he had responded with a name. Mo!

THE MURDER

A few months had passed. All the recent experiences she had gone through with Andrei and Mo, Louise had started to become even more anxious than ever. She began to believe people were out watching her and was going to harm her.

She was experiencing severe trauma from past events. Whenever she left the house, she would take a knife with her to protect her from people following her and from any possible harm. She would also sleep in bed with the knife under her pillow for safety. Lucian never knew about this!

She then started to hear people talking to her, whispering about her and hearing the voices making plans to kill her. Barricading herself in her house, she began placing items such as chairs and tables in front of her bedroom door every night—double-checking locks. She was in constant fear as if people were watching her.

Lucian saw his loving, and kind-hearted girlfriend become a nervous wreck. He had to continually reassure her she was safe, but this was not enough for her. She was riddled in fear every day. No sleep, she stopped eating and was always on edge for any slight noise she heard.

She was always on the lookout.

Lucian took Louise to the shopping mall for some groceries, holding hands as they always did. Walking across the market square, there was someone they recognised, Andrei.

He was sitting on a bench by himself, holding a can of beer. Louise could smell cheap beer three feet from his seat. There were not many people around. Andrei did not see them both because he had his back to them. Very quickly, Louise instantly felt fear. She started hearing The Voices again. She heard a whisper telling her Andrei was going to kill her. The voice told her he would follow her and stab her.

She was shaking and sweating extremely to a point, her hands were wet. Lucian also was nervous to see Andrei and felt anger. The last time he saw Andrei was that New Year's night.

Louise got defensive, and in one rapid second, she let loose of Lucian's hand and quickly walked towards Andrei. Lucian was behind her, pleading to stay away and trying to grab her, but she resisted.

Just as she went close behind Andrei, she suddenly pulled out a 6-inch kitchen knife that she had always carried with her since the incident. The Knife went straight through Andrei's right side of his neck! Andrei screamed in pain, holding on to his neck and fell forward to the ground on his left hand. He looked up to see Louise standing above him, holding the knife full of blood in her right hand.

Lucian was in shock; he did not have a clue what to do but to call the ambulance. He feared more for Louise's actions that she would be locked up for murder. Louise had blood on her hands; she was looking lost and confused. She had never hurt anyone in her life before. This was not her character at all, and Louise could not believe her eyes. What had she become? She could never think of hurting a small creature, yet killing a man. Louise shook her head in traumatisation.

Police and paramedics arrived at the scene and arrested Louise. Andrei was dead on the spot. Now Louise was being investigated for murder. Lucian had lost the love of his life. He was broken and torn, knowing this was not the Louise he knew. She had not been the same person for a long time since the sexual assault by Andrei.

Many investigations were made and enquiries by Police. Lucian was also questioned many times. She was later charged with murder!

Being held in prison while awaiting trial, Louise did not cope well at all. Still hearing voices and feeling fear of people. Doctors and psychiatrists started to assess her mental health and monitored her very closely. This took some time to evaluate and come to any conclusions about her behaviour. Although they were provided with her previous record of illnesses, this was something more serious.

Lucian visited her as often as possible and wrote every single day to her. He awaited replies but never got any. He still did not give up on her and wrote more. Tom lived with his dad, whereas Lucian looked after Louise's home while she was away. After a few weeks into her being put away, she called Lucian on the phone. Louise was explaining that *The Voices* told her to do it, that Andrei was going to kill her if Louise did not kill him first. Lucian was saddened to hear her frustration and to realise she needed help fast. Louise sometimes wrote to Tom, her son. She hoped that Lucian would be taking good care of him.

8 months after the murder of Andrei, Louise was found to have a mental health condition and diagnosed with bipolar and paranoid schizophrenia. This explained a lot about her behaviour and the reasons for hearing voices. She was hallucinating. Hearing and seeing people who were not there.

She needed mental help fast. The trial at court took this on board and dropped all charges of murder. She was mentally unwell, and her actions were not under her control. She was sectioned. When she stabbed Andrei, she was mentally incapable and was unaware of her actions. This meant she would stay in a mental hospital to be treated for her current diagnosis. This was a hard time for Lucian. Nonetheless, he felt relieved for her illness diagnosis and for the provision of mental help.

2 years later, after many trials of medications and having to do multiple therapies, Louise was allowed to go home. She still needed regular visits to check if she was managing to be back in the outside world, and she had her partner Lucian to support her.

She found herself always scared and afraid of being alone again because she did not want this sensation to end. *Lucian shows her what love is*, and the way he displayed was fantastic. How much affection he had was incredible and the most amazing and unique love that she had never had before. Louise was very infatuated. Every day, longing to touch and kiss him with all the passion inside. Lucian was lovesick to the happiness that he made her feel. Worshipping the ground, her lover walked on and adored her always.

Lucian had given her strength and power. How Louise felt for him was something that words could not describe. When he was beside her, she was happy and had a glare in her eyes. He gave her a powerful feeling deep inside the heart. This is what love does. He had lightened up her life, given so much hope and taught Louise how to become a better person. She was who she was because of him.

With Lucian, she felt safe and secure. Trusted him to protect her and the family. Louise imagined that he would not let anything or anyone destroy what they have. This bond and family that they had together was unbreakable. They believed in each other and had faith that they would make it to the end TO-GETHER. Loving him for as long as the stars are in the sky and more.

She craved his attention; felt addicted to him, and will always thank him for standing by her side when days were grey. Because they both felt the exact same way for each other and expressed their love in many ways, friends and family could see it. Their passion and devotion are not only for them but for others too.

People often say that they would love to have what Louise and Lucian got together. Some people have even become jealous. Some have tried to come between them, due to their jealousy. They do not want to see Louise and Lucian happy because those people are not.

Emil and his family had left the country to avoid investigations. Whatever Andrei, Mo, and Emil were trying to do to them that New Year's evening, it did not work out. Consequently, it goes to show really just how much of a strong bond Louise and Lucian genuinely have together.

It is understood, Louise was now Impervious.

I never knew

I needed you

Until in like

A hurricane

You blew

Picked me up

Swept me off

My feet

I got so lost

In eyes that deep

Drowning

Floundering

And you caught me

As I fell

Your girl

And right then

I knew I wanted

To be your life

Your wife

Different cultures

Different age

Different experiences

But felt the same pain

Dare I trust you again?

Yes

I knew I wanted

To be your life

Your wife

We lived in a bubble

Couldn't foresee the coming trouble

The storm born of

Jealousy formed

His chosen family really

Really hurt me

A party to celebrate

The love we have found,

Inviting his people round

Oblivious, I was,

To the sneaky hand

In the velvet glove

Disguising assault

As affection

An evil misdirection

To confuse, use and divide

Thank fuck for the phone that recorded

The wrong actions, uncalled for

And oh-so unwarranted

Recorded stopped

My truth from being distorted

And though this battle

Is still being fought

We have already won the war

Our love strong

You just strengthened

Our bond

And for that

I thank you

Michelle Emma Tobias

THE CONSENT

H ave you ever been in a situation where you have been asked to do something or made to feel obliged to act on something that you do not want to?

How many times do women go to bars and drink irresponsibly, only to find themselves taken home by strangers? A person that they have just met and suddenly become sexually active? When is a woman's consent to have sex with another person? Was it actually given freely and genuinely accepted as Consent?

Here, I want to share what I have researched and learnt through my own experiences that what I thought was Consent really is not. Whether you are married, dating, or just met someone on one night out, if a person asks you if you want to have sex or touches you sexually and you do not want that, you have a right to say NO.

If a person asks for sex and you say "No", but he still carries on asking and trying to tempt you. You feel pressured, but you continue to mean no, and you may refuse politely. He still compels you, and after saying, 'No', many more times, in one moment you feel obliged. The refusal turns to a "Yes", just because you have given in and are fed up of being asked repeatedly. You wish to shut him up to make him stop asking you again because he will not listen to the word "No", this still does not count as Consent. And in the eyes of the Law, it is sexual assault or rape. This is what many men do not know about and can land themselves in a tough situation with the Law.

Consent means agreeing freely, not when you are being forced or made to feel you have to have sex. It does not matter if the person you say No to, is your partner, husband, or someone you met on a night out. A No is No, and you are not giving Consent. Just because you said yes to going to the bedroom or agreed to attend to a person's home, does not mean you answered yes to having sex or even being touched. This includes feeling the woman's body, oral sex, or intercourse.

Remember that Consent is always reversible if at any time you change your mind about doing anything. Even if you have done it before or are both naked, you can still say 'No', and stop. At this point, you have not given further Consent. If you have answered yes and consented to sex, then after you are not comfortable and want to stop, you are entitled to assert NO. *The Consent is revocable.* You can change your mind at any time, and if the other person does not stop when you ask, then this is sexual harassment or assault.

Besides, when someone is under the influence of alcohol and drugs and agrees by saying yes to sex, this still is not consenting. Because they do not have an evident mentality to be able to make decisions freely. Again, the other person can be liable for rape or sexual assault!

Understand what Consent really means, and it is to be given by you freely. Besides, both partners need to give Consent. Only do what you want to do and be comfortable with it. Do not do what you feel you are expected to do. If your partner says "NO" (does not say anything or give an answer), then you still do not have Consent. If your partner says "YES" but looks unsure or uncomfortable, again, you do not have permission. You may not carry on the act without their full permission in their senses. There are Laws in place on who can and cannot give Consent. Moreover, Law protects minors under the age of 18 from being pressurised into sex with someone else of an older age.

Message to all the women

The most important thing is that approval is necessary for all the actions, which involve your body and your belongings. You own your body, and no one has the right to film any part of it without your Consent. If you detect a similar issue, report it to cyber-crime authorities who can trace the actions of that pervert. They will also remove your pictures or videos from any websites where the culprits had posted. You must contain a proof of their alleged activity because, in Louise's case, the evidence was not enough. The camera did not describe the scene well. Moreover, there was no record found in Mo's and Andrei's mobiles because they had already changed their phones. If you doubt anyone about sharing your videos or pictures, take prompt action without them knowing about it and catch the culprit in time.

FOLLOW CARIS POYNTER

ON HER FACEBOOK GROUP:

facebook.com/CWTTD

SHARE YOUR STORY ON

CARIS POYNTER EMAIL:

carishoughton@yahoo.co.uk

BOOKS BY THIS AUTHOR

THE FOUR TICCSTERS

Getting the right diagnosis for your kids' mental health is the hardest part. If your Kids show Tics and you cannot get the correct diagnosis, you are in the same boat as I was. My children started showing Tics and indicators of other Disorders gradually. It was my Son Ramani, who was the first, not the eldest, who showed symptoms from the age of four, and it took me eight years to get the proper judgment. I was shattered and confused, not knowing what comes next, worried about the health of my children, overcoming my Bipolar and OCD. It was too much for me as a mother.

I researched and studied for the sake of my kids. I achieved the Level 4 Diploma for Counselling and Certification of Training in Mentoring. I wanted to make a difference by helping others with Addiction. Therefore, I wrote this book with a passion for reaching out to everyone with similar problems.

It is my humble effort to raise awareness of Mental Disorders. Identification of the symptoms is the first age, ready for my story, and you will come to know about the effort it takes to figure out the problem finally. I have developed ways of my methods from research, action plan from experience to fight it out. Only then can we overcome those. Ignoring the signs in your loved ones will bring you no good; it is time to face it!

The Four Boys Tic Path that you are about to read is based on my experience and life's journey. I have shared specific events and the feelings related to those moments to explain the difficulty. If you equip yourself with the suggestions provided, you will likely loosen up your shoulders and focus on what is required out of you. Take action, Intervene early, Know my story!

THE FOUR MUSCULA'TEERS

Kathleen's life is full of daily struggles and medical conditions. Her life was about to change when she gave birth to four girls, three girls were diagnosed with Muscular Dystrophy, and the eldest one was a carrier of the disease. Her girls would outrun her in death, and she had to let go of each soul with excruciating pain.

The Four Muscula'teers is a story of a mother's life-long journey and what she had to go through. It is a tale of losing strength, losing beauty, losing laughter, losing your loved ones, losing muscles, losing wellbeing, losing family, and losing a life.

A woman hero, who fought all her life to provide care for her children and grandchildren, who had to see them go one by one. Kathy had four girls named Susan, Christine, Lorraine and the youngest one, Julie. They lived a happy family life, until...

Follow Caris Poynter's

YouTube Channel

TSKIDS Children with Tourettes and Tics

*https://www.youtube.com/channel/
UCSOIS93hWxMeI5fb4OwnMEg/*

ABOUT THE AUTHOR

CARIS POYNTER

Caris Poynter is a Mentor, Philanthropist. As a writer, Ms Poynter is passionate about Tourette's, Muscular Dystrophy and Other Health Issues. Being a mother herself, she wants to reach out to the parents from-all-walks-of-life to raise awareness regarding Children Health and Social Issues.

Printed in Poland
by Amazon Fulfillment
Poland Sp. z o.o., Wrocław

61506560R00059